Drawing Fun

HOW TO DRAW Mythical CREATURES

by Kathryn Clay

illustrated by Anne Timmons

Capstone press

Mankato, Minnesota

Snap Books are published by Capstone Press,
151 Good Counsel Drive, P.O. Box 669, Mankato, Minnesota 56002.
www.capstonepress.com

Library of Congress Cataloging-in-Publication Data
Clay, Kathryn.
    How to draw mythical creatures / by Kathryn Clay; illustrated by Anne Timmons.
    p. cm. — (Snap. Drawing fun)
    Includes bibliographical references and index.
    Summary: "Lively text and fun illustrations describe how to draw mythical creatures" — Provided by publisher.
    ISBN-13: 978-1-4296-2307-0 (hardcover)
    ISBN-10: 1-4296-2307-1 (hardcover)
    1. Art and mythology — Juvenile literature. 2. Animals, Mythical, in art — Juvenile literature. 3. Drawing —
Technique — Juvenile literature. I. Timmons, Anne. II. Title. III. Series.
NC825.M9C53 2009
743'.87 — dc22   2008035002

Credits
Juliette Peters, designer
Abbey Fitzgerald, colorist

Photo Credits
Capstone Press/TJ Thoraldson Digital Photography, 4 (pencil), 5 (all), 32 (pencil)

The author dedicates this book to Matt, a big fan of unicorns and mythical worlds.

1 2 3 4 5 6 14 13 12 11 10 09

Table of Contents

Getting Started

You already draw just about everything in sight. To you, a blank sheet of paper is just another canvas. That's why every scrap of paper in your room is covered with sketches. With your talent and these step-by-step instructions, you can turn those sketches into amazing works of art.

Maybe you want to draw mythical animals? Practice drawing the graceful Pegasus. Would you rather work on ugly monsters? Try sketching Medusa and her serpent hair. Are you really into fairy-tale figures? Then check out the mischievous woodland elf.

Of course, there are all kinds of mythical creatures. Once you've mastered some of the creatures in this book, you'll be able to draw your own fantasy figures. Let your imagination run wild, and see what kind of mythical creatures you can create.

Must-Have Materials

1. First you'll need something to draw on.
   Any blank, white paper will work well.

2. Pencils are a must for these drawing projects.
   Be sure to keep a bunch nearby.

3. Because sharp pencils make clean lines,
   you'll be sharpening those pencils a lot.
   Have a pencil sharpener handy.

4. Even the best artist needs to erase a line now
   and then. Pencil erasers wear out fast. A rubber
   or kneaded eraser will last much longer.

5. To make your drawings pop off the page,
   use colored pencils or markers.

Fairy

According to legend, fairies love to visit humans. Sometimes they come as twinkling spots of light in a dark room. Other times you might feel a soft breeze against your cheek as you drift off to sleep.

Once you've mastered this fairy, add a few more fairies dancing in the moonlight.

STEP 1

STEP 2

STEP 3

STEP 4

7

Genie

This genie has been stuck in a bottle for a long, long time. Now he's free and looking for work. If you're lucky, he might just grant you a wish or two.

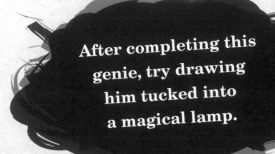

After completing this genie, try drawing him tucked into a magical lamp.

STEP 1

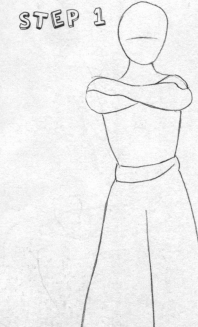

STEP 2

STEP 3

STEP 4

Mermaid

Mermaids are nearly impossible to see. They stay hidden below the waves in the deepest part of the ocean. If you happen to catch a quick glimpse, you might mistake her for a beautiful woman. But a closer look will prove there's something fishy about her.

After completing this mermaid, try to draw her swimming with a school of fish.

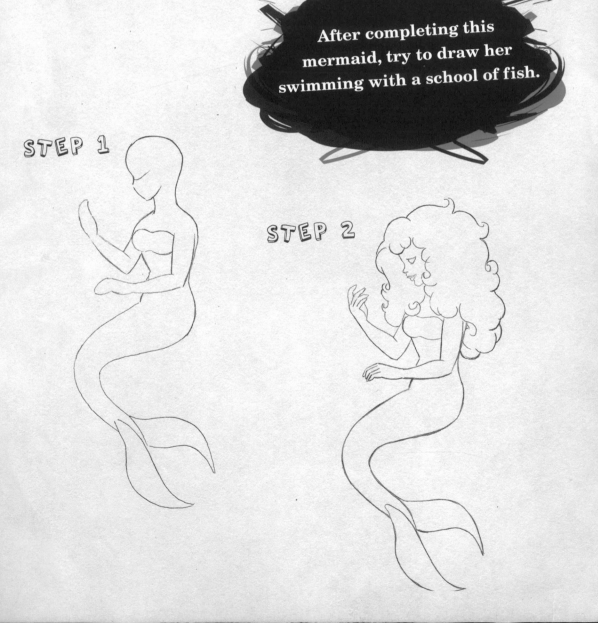

STEP 1

STEP 2

STEP 3

STEP 4

Dragon

Someone dared to disturb this sleeping dragon. Now he's awake and angry. Watch out! There's no knight in shining armor to protect you. If this dragon decides to use his fiery breath, you could be toast!

Dragons are always looking for castles to attack. Try drawing an enchanted castle surrounded by a moat.

STEP 1

STEP 2

STEP 3

STEP 4

13

Good Witch

You won't find any warts or broomsticks near this witch. That's because she's a good witch. She's not interested in turning people into frogs or casting evil spells. She'd rather use her powers to help others.

This witch has suddenly turned wicked. Draw her with crooked teeth and a long, pointy nose.

STEP 1

STEP 2

STEP 3

STEP 4

Woodland Elf

Next time you're in a forest, keep a close eye out for these tiny creatures. Woodland elves stay hidden in the trees. If you wait long enough, you might see one resting on a toadstool.

After finishing this elf, sketch a tree where she can hide.

STEP 1

STEP 2

Medusa

Medusa was a beautiful woman before the Greek goddess Athena turned her into a monster. Now you better watch out for her terrifying tresses. Stare at them too long, and you might turn to stone!

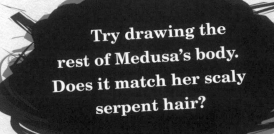

Try drawing the rest of Medusa's body. Does it match her scaly serpent hair?

STEP 1

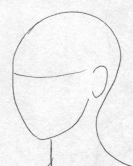

STEP 2

STEP 3

STEP 4

Pegasus

According to Greek mythology, this winged horse is the son of Poseidon and Medusa. But unlike his mother, Pegasus managed to escape Athena's evil spell. Draw him flying through the clouds with his legs in mid-gallop.

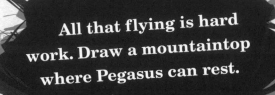

All that flying is hard work. Draw a mountaintop where Pegasus can rest.

STEP 1

STEP 2

STEP 3

STEP 4

Garden Pixie

Garden pixies rarely roam from their flower-filled homes. They spend their days asleep on the soft petals of pansies. At night, they dance among the flower buds like bees.

Now try drawing a flower garden filled with pixies.

STEP 1

STEP 2

STEP 3

STEP 4

Unicorn

With a touch of its glowing horn, a unicorn can heal anyone who is hurting. Maybe that's why people spend so much time chasing after these amazing animals.

After mastering this drawing, try sketching a unicorn running across a colorful rainbow.

STEP 1

STEP 2

STEP 3

STEP 4

Magical Friends

Your best friend probably can't run across rainbows or heal the injured with a touch of her horn. This fairy is lucky enough to have found such a friend. Of course, these are just the perks of being friends with a unicorn.

Try drawing this playful pair racing against Pegasus.

STEP 1

STEP 2

STEP 3

To finish this drawing, turn to the next page. ⇨

STEP 4

STEP 5

Glossary

Athena (uh-THEE-nuh) — the goddess of wisdom and war in Greek mythology

legend (LEJ-uhnd) — a story handed down from earlier times; legends are often based on fact, but they are not entirely true.

moat (MOHT) — a deep, wide ditch dug all around a castle, fort, or town and filled with water to prevent attacks

mythology (mi-THOL-uh-jee) — a collection of myths

Poseidon (puh-SIGH-dun) — the god of the sea in Greek mythology

serpent (SUR-puhnt) — a snake

toadstool (TOHD-stool) — a wild mushroom

Read More

Beaumont, Steve. *How to Draw Magical Kings and Queens*. Drawing Fantasy Art. New York: PowerKids Press, 2008.

Bergin, Mark. *Magical Creatures and Mythical Beasts*. How to Draw. New York: Rosen, 2009.

Soloff-Levy, Barbara. *How to Draw Wizards, Dragons, and Other Magical Creatures*. Mineola, N.Y.: Dover Publications, 2004.

Internet Sites

FactHound offers a safe, fun way to find educator-approved Internet sites related to this book.

Here's what you do:
1. Visit *www.facthound.com*
2. Choose your grade level.
3. Begin your search.

This book's ID number is 9781429623070.

FactHound will fetch the best sites for you!

Index